First edition published in 2014
This edition published in Great Britain in 2023 by Singing Dragon,
an imprint of Jessica Kingsley Publishers
An imprint of Hodder & Stoughton Ltd
An Hachette Company

1

A CIP catalogue record for this title is available from the British Library
and the Library of Congress

ISBN 978 1 83997 533 2
eISBN 978 1 83997 532 5

Printed and bound in China by Leo Paper Products Limited

Jessica Kingsley Publishers' policy is to use papers that are natural,
renewable and recyclable products and made from wood grown in
sustainable forests. The logging and manufacturing processes are expected
to conform to the environmental regulations of the country of origin.

Jessica Kingsley Publishers
Carmelite House
50 Victoria Embankment
London EC4Y 0DZ

www.singingdragon.com

Sigrún Daníelsdóttir

Your Body is Awesome
Body Respect for Children

Illustrations and design by
Björk Bjarkadóttir

 SINGING DRAGON
LONDON AND PHILADELPHIA

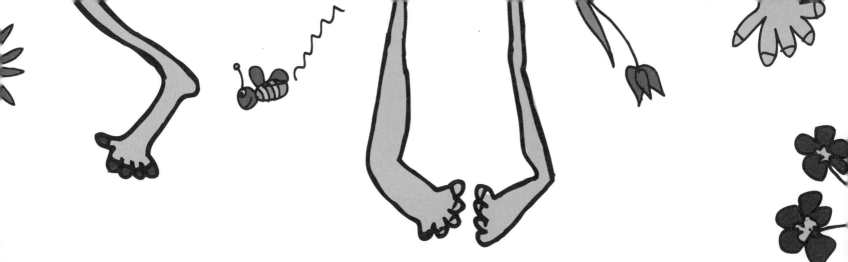

For my children:

Silja, Rökkvi and Pétur

Everybody has a body.

We live in our body.

It is like our house.

Bodies are amazing instruments that allow us to do all sorts of exciting things.

Like jumping up and down.
Dancing.
And splashing.

Bodies are fun.

Our bodies can make us feel good.

Like when we get a foot massage.

Or snuggle up on the sofa.

Or when someone strokes our back at bedtime.

It's nice to have a body.

Bodies are smart.

They let us know what they need to stay well and feel good.

Bodies don't use words to talk to us. They use feelings.
They send us messages about what they need through the
way we feel.

When we feel hungry, our body is telling us that it needs food.

GR...

When we feel full, our body is telling us that it has had enough for now.

It is important to listen to our bodies. What happens, for instance, if the body lets us know that it needs to go to the bathroom and we don't listen?

It is also important that adults listen to us when we tell them what is happening in our body. When we say that we are full, or tired, or need to use the bathroom, adults should listen. Our body knows best.

Try closing your eyes and traveling down into your tummy.

How do you feel in there? Is your stomach hungry?

Full? Or neither?

Stretch out your toes and fingers into every direction.

Try feeling your hands, your feet, your mouth and ears.

Feel the way the air comes down into your lungs through your mouth when you breathe deeply and then goes back out the same way.

This is your body. It is amazing.

Your body is brilliant.

It makes your heart beat and the blood pump through your veins.

It digests your food and grows bigger and stronger every day.

It makes your hair and nails grow, it heals your cuts and bruises, and fights illness and infections.

Your body is a good body.

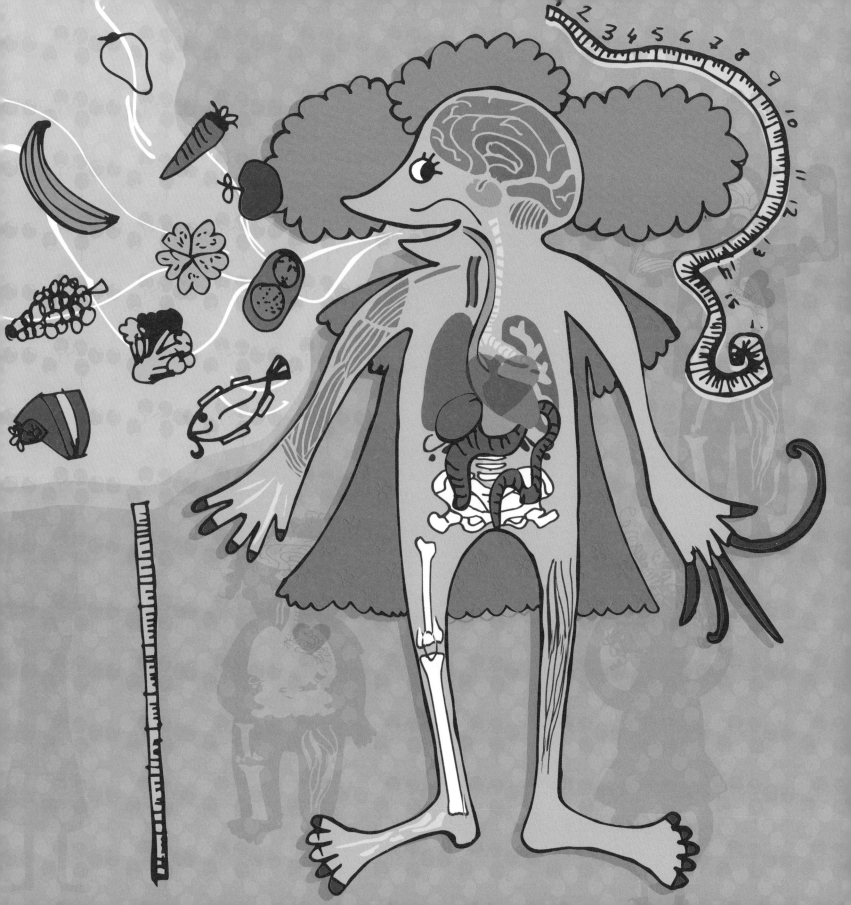

Bodies need a lot of care.

They need nutritious food to grow bigger and have the energy to do everything they need to do all day.

They need lots of fun and activity in order to stay healthy and have strong muscles and bones.

They need to get plenty of rest at night so that they will be refreshed and ready for action the next day.

And they need time, and sometimes help, to heal when they get sick or hurt.

Every body is different.

Some bodies are taller and others are shorter.

Some bodies are larger and others are smaller.

Some have curly hair and others straight.

Some have dark skin and others fair.

Every body is unique.

Just imagine if human beings were flowers. Wouldn't it be boring if all the flowers in the world were the same? We want to have all sorts of flowers so that we can make a beautiful, colorful, big bunch of flowers.

We also want there to be all sorts of birds and animals.

And we think it's much more fun to color with lots of crayons instead of just one.

It's wonderful that everything is so different.

All bodies are good bodies.

A tall body isn't better than a short body –
they are just different.

Fat and thin bodies are also different.
Neither is better than the other.
They are just different.

Like pink and green.

Or tulips and daisies.

It is important to feel good about your body and be happy about the way you are.

It's also important to allow others to be happy about the way they are.

We don't need to be like anybody but ourselves.

Be kind to your body and treat it with love.

Your body is your friend and you will live in it all your life.

A MESSAGE FOR ADULTS

This book is written for children and the adults who care for them in the hope of promoting healthy body image and respect for diversity. Children's body image is part of their general self-image and therefore it is important that they grow up in an environment that helps them see their bodies in a positive way. Even though it is obvious that bodies come in different shapes and sizes, and have different abilities, we live in an environment that doesn't always respect this fact. As a result, many people feel uncomfortable in their skin and think they should be different from how they are.

Children's body image has a powerful influence on their health and well-being. Young people who are dissatisfied with their bodies are at an increased risk of having lower self-esteem and various health problems. We take better care of the things we love and so it is important for children to learn to love their bodies from the very start.

For children to be able to develop a positive body image, their bodies need to be appreciated in the world around them. That is why body diversity needs to be embraced as a normal part of life and met with the same respect and inclusion we try to promote in other areas of human diversity. We should speak openly to children about all bodies being different and teach them that this diversity is a natural and positive aspect of human existence.

We also want children to learn that their bodies are precious and need care. It is important for them to get to know their bodies, maintain curiosity about them, and learn to listen and respond to the signals their bodies send them. These are things children need to learn on their own terms, guided by self-care. Children should never be led to believe that there is something wrong with their bodies or the bodies of others.

All children have the right to feel good in their skin and be proud of themselves the way they are. That should be regarded among the most fundamental of children's rights.

ABOUT THE ILLUSTRATOR

Björk Bjarkadóttir was born in Iceland but is now living in Oslo. Her current projects include writing children's books, illustration, graphic design and photography.

For more information,
www.bjorkbjarka.no

Sigrún Daníelsdóttir is a psychologist specializing in body image and eating issues. She believes all bodies are created equal and kids should be supported in being happy in their own, unique skin.